Contents

All words marked in **bold** are explained in
the glossary.

BRITAIN

Londinium *(London)*

GERMANY

Colonia Agrippina
(Cologne)

Lutetia *(Paris)*

Rhine

Danube

GAUL

ITALY

ILLYRIA

SPAIN

Tiber

Roma *(Rome)*

Carthago *(Carthage)*

MAURETANIA

Mediterranean Sea

The Roman World

THE ROMANS

by Peter Chrisp

Editorial Consultant: Dr Jamie Masters,
Research Fellow in Classics,
Clare College, Cambridge

First published in Great Britain in 1993 by
Two-Can Publishing
a division of Zenith Entertainment plc
43-45 Dorset Street
London W1H 4AB

© Two-Can Publishing, 1993
Edited by Mike Hirst and Deborah Kespert
Designed by Fionna Robson

Printed in Hong Kong

6 8 10 9 7

A catalogue record for this book is available from
the British Library.

HBK ISBN: 1 85434 214 2
PBK ISBN: 1 85434 215 0

Photographic Credits
Ancient Art and Architecture Collection: p9 (top right), p10, p19 (top left), p20;
Bridgeman Art Library: p14 (bottom right), p21 (bottom right), p23;
Bruce Coleman: p17, p30 (bottom right);
C.M. Dixon: p13, p14 (top right), p21 (top left); E.T. Archive: p9;
Michael Holford: p12, p16, p19 (bottom), p24, p30 (left), p30 (top right); Zefa: p7.

Illustration Credits
Gillian Hunt: pp 4—24
Maxine Hamil: cover, pp 25—29

Between around 300 BC and AD 200, the people of Rome built up a huge **empire**. It included all of the lands surrounding the Mediterranean Sea and was one of the best-organized empires in history. It lasted for hundreds of years.

Throughout their Empire, the Romans built cities and roads. In the conquered lands, people learnt to live like the Romans – to wear Roman clothes, worship Roman gods and speak Latin, the Roman language. People who had been living in small villages began to live in cities too.

The Romans firmly believed that their own way of life was the best in the world. They thought they were doing the peoples they conquered a favour by showing them the proper way to live.

Byzantium *(Istanbul)*

ACEDONIA

ASIA MINOR

Athenae *(Athens)*

GREECE

Euphrates

Tigris

SYRIA

Hierosolyma *(Jerusalem)*

Alexandria

EGYPT

Nile

Goods from all over the Empire were brought to Rome by ship. Olives came from Spain, for example, and corn was harvested in Egypt.

The City of Rome

At the heart of the Roman Empire was the great city of Rome, a place where more than one million people lived. For anyone living in the Empire, this was the centre of the world.

The city was full of grand public buildings – temples, theatres, public baths and sports arenas. The streets were lined with statues of Rome's greatest men, and with decorated arches, built to celebrate victories in war.

However, Rome also had many slum districts, where the poorer people lived in overcrowded blocks of flats, separated by narrow, dark alleys.

The Colosseum

Temple of Caesar

The Sacred Way

This is the Forum, as it looked in the first century AD. The Forum was the main centre of government, business, law and religion in Rome. Public meetings were held here and great religious ceremonies took place.

Arch of Titus

Temple of Vesta

Temple of Castor and Pollux

Basilica Julia

▲ The Roman Forum as it looks today. Can you spot the remains of any buildings shown in the drawing?

This is how one Roman writer, called Seneca, described the great capital city where he lived:

'Look at the crowds! They come here from all over the world. Some come for entertainment, others have come to make their fortunes.'

Republic and Emperors

For almost 500 years, until 27 BC, Rome was a **republic**. It was ruled by elected officials rather than by a single person. The most important officials, chosen each year, were the two **Consuls.** They ruled with the advice of the **Senate,** a council made up of men from Rome's most important families.

The republican way of ruling the Empire broke down during a series of terrible **Civil Wars** – wars in which one section of the Roman Army battled against another. The wars were caused by a group of ambitious generals and politicians, who fought among themselves for power.

The final victor in the Civil Wars was Augustus. He made himself more powerful than the Consuls and Senate and became the first of the emperors. These men would rule in Rome for the next five centuries. There were more than a hundred emperors in all.

▼ During the Civil Wars, Julius Caesar, who was a successful general and politician, became ruler of Rome. For five years, he was the most powerful man in the Empire, but in 44 BC he was killed by a group of senators. However, even after Caesar's death, the Civil Wars continued for another thirteen years.

▲ Rome's first emperor, Augustus. Later Romans thought that he was an ideal ruler.

Augustus (27 BC–AD 14)

Augustus was a cautious ruler who gave Rome peace after the bloody Civil Wars. During his reign of more than forty years, the Roman people got used to being ruled by one man. He encouraged the building of many new roads, bridges and temples. After his death, the Senate declared that Augustus had become a god.

Hadrian (AD 117–138)

Hadrian was one of the hardest-working Roman emperors. He spent years travelling all over the Empire, strengthening the frontiers with forts and walls, such as the one he built across northern Britain. When he was not travelling, he was busy changing the laws of Rome. Some of his laws protected slaves from cruel treatment.

▲ These coins show an emperor visiting London, and a new harbour at Ostia, close to Rome.

Coins

Roman coins were not just objects for buying things. They often carried a portrait of the emperor to show people throughout the Empire what their ruler looked like. A coin was also like a small newspaper, announcing great events, such as the building of a new temple in Rome. Other coins praised the emperor's generosity or wise rule.

▲ The Emperor Augustus watches over the building of a new temple in Rome.

The Roman Army

It was thanks to the Army that the Romans were able to conquer and protect their huge Empire. The Roman Army was successful because it was better organized, better trained and better disciplined than any other army of the time.

The Army was divided into **legions**, each of around 5,500 men. Every legion had a number and a nickname, 'Victorious' or 'Lightning', for example. Soldiers were proud to belong to their own legion.

A Roman soldier was a real professional. He would serve in the legion for twenty-five years, living in barracks or a fort with his fellow soldiers. Much of his time was spent training – practising with weapons, or going on long marches loaded with heavy equipment.

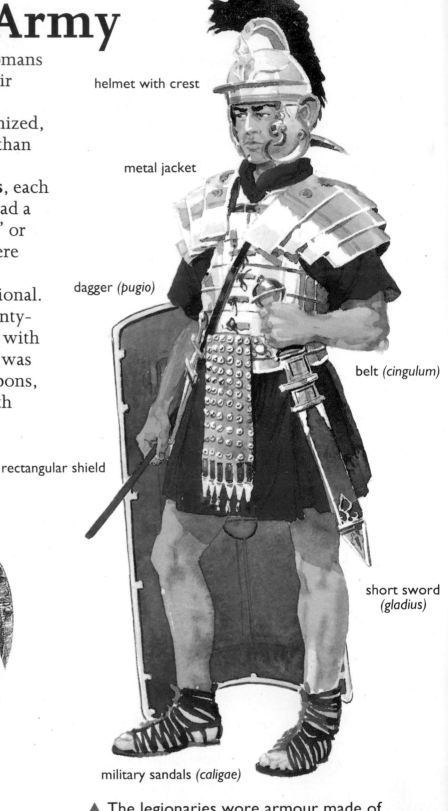

helmet with crest

metal jacket

dagger (*pugio*)

belt (*cingulum*)

rectangular shield

short sword (*gladius*)

military sandals (*caligae*)

▲ The legionaries wore armour made of overlapping plates of metal, which let them bend freely. The helmet crest was only worn for special occasions such as parades.

▲ An officer's decorated helmet

A Roman Camp

When they were on the march, soldiers would have to build a fresh camp each evening. It would be a rectangular shape, protected by a ditch and an earth bank lined with wooden stakes. Inside the camp, the soldiers pitched their tents in neat rows.

One Roman writer explained the importance of Army camps:

'If a camp is properly built, the soldiers spend their days and nights safe and sound. It is as though they carried a fortified city around with them wherever they go.'

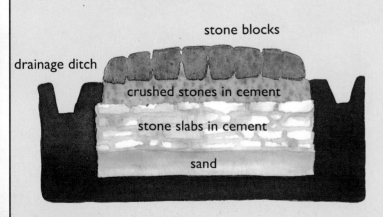

Building Roads

drainage ditch

stone blocks

crushed stones in cement

stone slabs in cement

sand

When they were not training, fighting or marching, the soldiers were kept busy quarrying stone and building roads. These roads were always as straight as possible, so that the Army could travel quickly from one part of the Empire to another. The Romans preferred to tunnel through a hill rather than take the long way around it. However, the ordinary soldiers hated road building and grumbled about it in their letters.

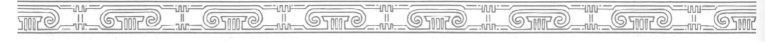

Slaves

Roman society was divided into different social classes. The most powerful people were **citizens**. They were men who had many rights, and could vote in elections.

Slaves were much worse off. They had no rights and were owned by their masters. If they tried to run away they were often whipped, branded with a hot iron, and sometimes even killed.

Many Romans had slaves to do their hard and dirty work for them. These slaves could be bought and sold in the market place.

Some slaves were prisoners, captured in war. Others were the children of slave parents or orphans who had been brought up by slave traders.

Slavery was an accepted part of life in Roman times. Some Romans said that slaves should be treated kindly, but no one thought that slavery itself was wrong.

▼ When rich Romans went out, their slaves would carry them through the streets in a small carriage surrounded by curtains, called a litter.

▲ Slaves often had to wear metal tags in case they escaped. This one says, 'Hold me, lest I flee, and return me to my master Viventius.'

Gladiators

Some slaves and criminals were forced to become gladiators – men who fought to the death in public entertainments.

These fights were hugely popular. The crowds would cheer on their favourite gladiators. When the first blood was drawn, they would cry, 'He's got him!' Gladiators who won fight after fight became as famous as film stars are today. But few of them ever lived to be old men.

▲ An African slave pours a bowl of wine for a Roman. Many Romans were not very tall, and slaves from places outside Italy, such as Germany and Africa, were often bigger and stronger than the Romans. But these slaves still had to take orders from their Roman masters.

Household Slaves

Wealthy Romans had dozens of slaves working in their households. Slaves would help them get dressed, cook for them, entertain them and clean up after them. The most highly-prized slaves were Greeks, for they were often better educated than their Roman masters. They served as doctors, tutors and secretaries.

The Romans came to rely so much on their slaves that they would often treat them as members of the family. Slaves who served their masters well might one day be lucky enough to be rewarded with their freedom.

▲ As well as fighting each other, gladiators were also made to fight wild animals such as lions and bears. The animals were brought to Rome from all over the Empire.

▲ A gladiator's dagger.

Gods and Temples

The Romans worshipped many different gods and goddesses. Each of the gods controlled a different part of life. Jupiter was the most powerful of the gods. His wife, Juno, was the goddess of married women and watched over childbirth.

There were lesser gods for almost every other activity, as well as gods for places, such as hills, crossroads and fields. There was even one goddess, called Cardea, who watched over door hinges!

The most important gods had temples, buildings which housed their statues and which were looked after by official priests. People would bring gifts to a temple to ask the god a special favour. The most highly-prized gifts were the animals that were sacrificed – killed as an offering to the god.

▼ Most Roman houses had shrines. Here the gods who looked after the family would be given offerings of food each day.

▲ The Romans took many of their gods from the countries they conquered. This is Serapis, a sun and sky god, first worshipped in Egypt.

Christianity

The biggest change in Roman religion was the coming of Christianity. The Christians believed in just one god and they refused to worship any Roman gods. At first, the Christians were punished as criminals. But in AD 312 the Emperor Constantine himself was converted to the new religion.

▶ This jug is decorated with Christian symbols.

Signs from the Gods

The Romans believed that they could tell from special signs whether the gods were pleased or angry. One popular way of reading the signs was to examine the liver of a sacrificed animal. Another method was to offer some food to a flock of 'sacred chickens'. If the chickens refused to eat the food, it was a bad sign.

In the third century BC, a general called Claudius Pulcher took the sacred chickens to sea with him. He was so furious when they refused to eat, that he threw them overboard crying, 'If you won't eat, you'll drink instead!' Soon after, he suffered a terrible defeat. The Roman people blamed it on Pulcher's treatment of the chickens.

The Roman Baths

Every Roman town had at least one public bathhouse. Here, for a small sum, people would come each day to exercise, wash, chat and relax.

Men and women bathed separately. The bigger bathhouses had special areas for each sex. In the smaller baths, they would bathe at different times of the day.

Each bathhouse had a courtyard for exercise, such as weightlifting, wrestling or ball games. There was also a swimming pool and a number of rooms which were kept at different temperatures. Bathers sat and sweated in the hot room, where they could also take a hot bath. Then they might move to the cold room for a quick plunge in the cold water.

▼ The bathhouse needed a large staff of slaves, carrying towels, giving massages and stoking the furnaces to heat the water. The slaves would rub the bathers with olive oil (the Romans did not have soap). Then they would scrape them clean with a curved metal tool called a **strigil**.

cold room (*frigidarium*)

▶ Many bathers carried their own oil to the baths in jugs like this one.

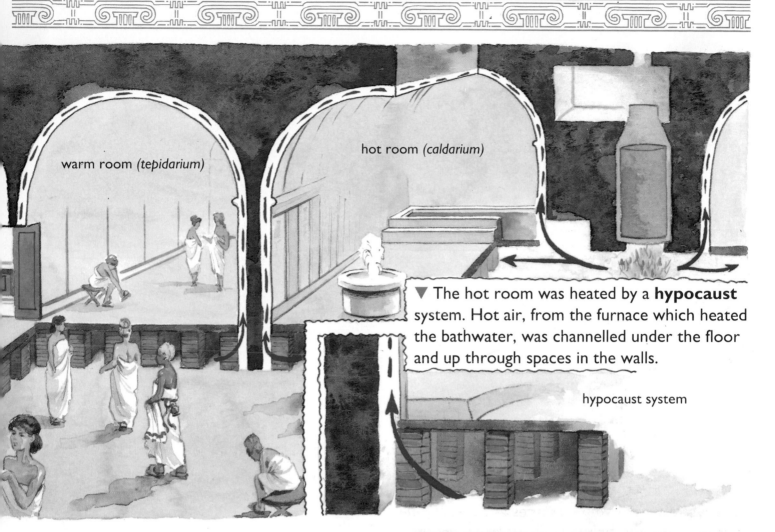

warm room (tepidarium)

hot room (caldarium)

▼ The hot room was heated by a **hypocaust** system. Hot air, from the furnace which heated the bathwater, was channelled under the floor and up through spaces in the walls.

hypocaust system

Not everyone was keen on the baths. One Roman writer thought they were a real nuisance, and complained about them in a letter to his friend:

'I live right above the public baths. Imagine the kinds of noise I have to put up with! There are the energetic types, heaving weights about with grunts and gasps. Next the lazy fellow having a cheap massage — I can hear the smack of a hand pummelling his shoulders. Then there's the man who always likes the sound of his own voice, and the others who leap into the pool with a huge splash. And think of the cries of the men selling drinks, sausages and pastries!'

▶ Roman towns used a lot of water, for both baths and houses. The water was brought to the towns along special channels called aqueducts.

Farming

Wealthy Romans were usually the owners of great farming estates. Each estate had a large workforce of slaves, watched over by a steward who was also a slave.

The most important crops were wheat, olives and grapes. Each farm had its own special building for making wine, and presses which crushed the olives to make oil. There were also workshops for the carpenters and blacksmiths, who repaired the farm tools and carts.

Other slaves looked after the cattle, sheep and pigs. The animals' manure kept the soil rich for the growing crops. Oxen were useful for pulling the plough and the cart which took the crops to the market place.

The slaves harvest corn and then thresh it – horses trample on the corn to separate the grains from their husks.

The Romans used pruning knives on their vines and olive trees.

A Farmer's Sacrifice

Throughout the year, Roman farmers had to perform religious rituals. They believed these rituals were just as important as sowing or ploughing at the right time. In May, for example, a pig, a ram and a bull would be led around the boundaries of the fields and then killed as a sacrifice to Mars.

How to Treat Your Slaves

Roman landowners didn't always agree about the best way to treat their slaves. Some people thought it was better to treat slaves kindly:

'The foremen will work harder if they are rewarded. They should be given a bit of property of their own, and mates from among their fellow-slaves to bear them children. This will make them more steady and more attached to the farm.'

But other landowners thought that their slaves were hardly more important than their animals:

'Sell worn-out oxen, worn-out tools, old slaves, sickly slaves and anything else that is no longer of any use.'

▼ This mosaic shows the gathering and treading of grapes, the first stage in wine making.

Food

Poor Romans lived on a very simple diet — porridge or bread made from wheat, soup made from millet or lentils, with onions, turnips, beans, figs, olives and sometimes pork, the cheapest meat.

In contrast, rich Romans could afford to buy food from all over the Empire. Different places were famous for their different products – Syria grew pears and Greece produced wine, for example.

A Roman Kitchen

Roman kitchens were usually small rooms, simply equipped. A charcoal fire heated a brick hearth. The cooks fried or boiled food in earthenware or bronze pots. For baking or roasting, they placed meat in the ashes of a small brick oven. The kitchen would also have large jars of olive oil, wine, vinegar and fish sauce, as well as a **mortar** for grinding up spices.

▼ The slaves are kept busy in the kitchen of a rich Roman's house, preparing a dinner party.

◄ Pottery like this was mass produced for Roman kitchens. These bowls come from Sussex in southern England.

▲ This mosaic shows a slave boy in the kitchen. Can you recognize the different foods?

A Dinner Party

Serving expensive and unusual food at a dinner party was a way of showing off wealth. Guests would eat lying down on couches, leaning on their left elbows while they picked at the food with their fingers. They often had to wash their hands during the meal.

Dinner had a number of courses. It started with an appetizer – salad, eggs, snails or shellfish, such as sea-urchins. This was served with **mulsum**, wine sweetened with honey.

Then the slaves brought out the main courses of fish and meat. Specialities included dormice stuffed with pork and pine kernels, sows' udders and roast peacock – the more unusual the food, the better. Finally there was a sweet course of cakes and fruit.

After the food had been eaten, the guests would often drink more, while they were entertained by singers, acrobats, clowns or story-tellers.

▲ The most popular Roman flavouring was **liquamen**, or fish sauce. It was made from anchovies or the insides of mackerel, which were soaked in salt water and left to rot in the sun. Liquamen was very spicy and salty.

A Roman House

From the outside, the houses of wealthy Romans looked very bare. They were designed to be private and safe from burglary, and so there were hardly any outside windows. Instead, Roman houses faced inwards. Each had a courtyard and a garden, with rooms arranged around them.

If you visited a Roman house, you would first go into the **atrium**, a sort of entrance hall or courtyard – since it had an opening in the ceiling to let in light. Beneath the opening was a basin which collected rainwater. Before aqueducts were built, bringing running water to the houses, this basin would have been the family's main water supply.

From the atrium, you would go into the **tablinum**, a sort of living room and office. This was where the head of the family would greet his daily visitors.

▼ A cut-away view of a Roman house.

bedroom

atrium

tablinum

peristyle

kitchen

Behind the tablinum was the garden, which was full of flowers and ornamental statues. The most popular type of garden, called a **peristyle**, had a covered walkway around its edges, giving shade on hot summer days.

Inside walls were covered with brightly-coloured paintings, showing gods and famous heroes, hunting and farming scenes, landscapes, animals, leaping fish and fighting gladiators. Floors were often decorated with mosaics – pictures made from hundreds of tiny tiles which had been pushed into the wet cement.

▶ A young woman picks flowers in this wall painting. The Romans loved paintings which reminded them of spring in the countryside.

Make a Mosaic

You can make a mosaic yourself, using squares of coloured paper instead of real tiles.

- Cut several sheets of different coloured paper into small squares.

- Sketch the outline of your mosaic in pencil on a sheet of plain paper.

- Then stick the coloured squares in place with paper glue.

- Remember to leave a tiny space between each of your paper 'tiles', so that the mosaic looks realistic.

Clothes

Men

Men wore a short wool or linen tunic. Over it, they sometimes wrapped a toga, a big plain woollen sheet, which was arranged in a complicated system of folds.

The toga was rather like a suit today. Men wore togas in public when they were meant to look smart. However, a toga was heavy, and took a long time to arrange properly. Away from Rome, most men normally preferred to wear just a simple cloak over their tunics.

Men were usually expected to be clean shaven. This meant a painful daily ordeal at the barbers, for the Romans did not use shaving soap. Even household slaves would be sent off to be shaved. It was a great relief for many men when the Emperor Hadrian decided to grow a beard and made shaving unfashionable.

▶ A wealthy Roman and his wife in smart dress.

Women

Women wore a much longer tunic which reached down to their ankles. On top they had a stola, a gown belted at the waist, and a broad cloak, often brightly coloured.

Hairstyles for wealthy women were always changing. Hair might be piled up as high as possible, or worn in tight ringlets.

Women also wore elaborate wigs. Some were jet black, made of hair imported from India. There were also blonde wigs, using hair clipped from German slave girls.

◀ Rich women wore beautiful jewellery set with precious stones, such as this necklace, bracelet and brooch.

Romulus and Remus

By the time the Romans came to write down their history, their city was already centuries old. But they told stories about their early years, to explain how their way of life came about. This story explains how the city was founded and why it was called 'Rome'.

Long ago, a wicked king called Amulius ruled over the city of Alba Longa. He had stolen the throne from his elder brother, Numitor, who fled to the hills and hid among the shepherds and herdsmen.

Amulius killed Numitor's two sons and forced Numitor's daughter to become a priestess. That way, she would never marry and have children who might take revenge on Amulius.

Nevertheless, one day Amulius was furious to hear that his niece had given birth to twin boys. She claimed that their father was Mars, the god of war, who had visited her one night in a dream.

Amulius did not believe her and ordered the two boys to be drowned. His servants set the babies afloat on the River Tiber in a reed basket. They drifted towards the Palatine Hill, and finally came to rest under a fig tree.

A she-wolf came across the babies, attracted by their crying. Instead of killing and eating them, she looked after the boys, feeding them with her own milk.

Soon after, an old shepherd called Faustulus was watching his flock when he noticed the fresh tracks of a wolf. Taking his spear, he set off to find the animal and kill it. To his amazement, he found the baby boys, along with the she-wolf, who was licking them clean with her tongue.

Faustulus took the babies home with him and showed them to his wife, Laurentia. The old shepherd and his wife had no children of their own, although they had always longed for some. So the couple decided they would bring up the boys themselves, and named them Romulus and Remus.

The twins grew up among the shepherds and herdsmen of the hills by the river Tiber. As they got older, they showed by their strength and cleverness that they were born leaders. The other boys all respected and looked up to them.

One day, a quarrel broke out between the twins and some herdsmen looking after the flocks belonging to Numitor. The herdsmen accused the twins of stealing cattle. There was a fight, and, in the scuffle, Remus was taken prisoner.

Numitor was puzzled when he met Remus. Something was strangely familiar about him. When Remus told Numitor his age and that he had a twin brother, the old man realized that he was talking to his own grandson! He was overjoyed. He told the twins who they really were, and how his wicked brother had wanted them dead.

Romulus and Remus agreed to help their grandfather get back the throne of Alba Longa. They led their fellow shepherds to the city and made a surprise attack on Amulius, killing him in his palace. Numitor was then welcomed back by the people of Alba Longa as the rightful king.

The twins were now princes in Alba Longa. But they were not happy there. They missed the hills on the River Tiber, where they had grown up. Eventually, they decided to go back there to found a city of their own.

Once they had reached the Tiber, the twins began to argue about where the city should be built. Remus said it should be on the Aventine Hill, but Romulus said they should choose the Palatine Hill, where they had been found by the she-wolf.

At last, the brothers decided to ask the gods to settle the question. Each of them stood on the hill he favoured and watched the sky for birds, signs from the gods. Soon a group of vultures began to circle, high up in the air. Six of them flew over Remus, who shouted, 'Look! The gods have chosen me!'

But then twelve of the vultures flew over Romulus. Romulus began to mark out the boundary line of his city, and his followers started digging a deep trench.

Remus watched with growing anger. He began to shout insults at his brother. For a while, Romulus ignored his brother's taunts, but when Remus and his followers started to jump over the boundary line, Romulus lost his temper. A fight broke out with picks and shovels. Remus was killed.

Instead of showing sadness at his brother's death, Romulus just said grimly, 'That's what will happen to anyone who tries to jump over my city walls!'

The new city was given the name of Rome, in honour of Romulus. He proved to be a wise king, and ruled over his people for thirty-eight years.

One day, while King Romulus was watching his soldiers parade on the Field of Mars, there was a sudden thunderstorm. A thick black cloud wrapped itself around him and, in a flash of lightning, he disappeared. The Romans said that their founder had gone to join his father Mars, up in the heavens.

How We Know

Have you ever wondered how we know so much about the Romans, even though they lived so long ago?

Evidence from Books

The Romans were great writers and many of their books and letters have survived. We can still read Roman poetry, plays and history books, as well as manuals on law, religion, warfare, farming and cookery.

▲ The scenes on mosaics have told us many things about everyday life in Roman times.

▲ The Arch of Titus in Rome. Since Roman times, many other victorious generals have built copies of Roman triumphal arches such as this.

Evidence Around Us

The Roman way of life still influences our own lives today. Lots of our words come from Latin, the Roman language. Planets and months of the year are still called by Roman names. We use the Roman alphabet too, and many of our buildings, as well as our coins, are modelled on Roman ones.

Evidence from the Ground

Many Roman buildings have been uncovered by archaeologists. The most spectacular discoveries were at the city of Pompeii, which was buried by ash and mud from the volcano Vesuvius in AD 79. The remains of the city were preserved for almost 1,800 years beneath the volcanic ash, so that today we can even tell what food was cooking on the stoves when the volcano suddenly erupted.

▲ Many people lost their lives at Pompeii. This boy was buried under the volcanic ash. When his body decayed, it left a space in the ash which archaeologists filled with plaster to make a cast.

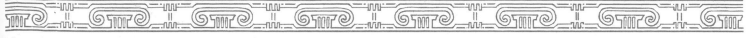

Glossary

Atrium The entrance hall of a large Roman house.

Citizen A member of a state. Roman citizens had more rights than people who lived in the Empire but were not citizens. Only citizens could stand for election, vote, or join the Army.

Civil War A war fought between people who belong to the same nation.

Consuls The two most important officals in the Roman government under the republic.

Empire A large area with many different peoples, all ruled by a single government.

Hypocaust A type of central heating, using hot air channelled under the floors, which were held up on brick columns.

Legion A Roman Army made up of around 5,500 men.

Liquamen A popular Roman sauce made from rotten fish.

Mortar A stone bowl that is used for grinding spices.

Mulsum A Roman drink made from wine and sweetened with honey.

Peristyle The garden of a Roman house with a covered walkway around its edges.

Republic A state ruled by elected officials instead of a king or emperor.

Senate Roman governing council, made up of the heads of the most important families. It gave advice to the Consuls and, later, to the emperor.

Strigil A metal tool used for scraping dirty oil off the skin.

Tablinum The most important room in a Roman house, a reception room and office.

Index

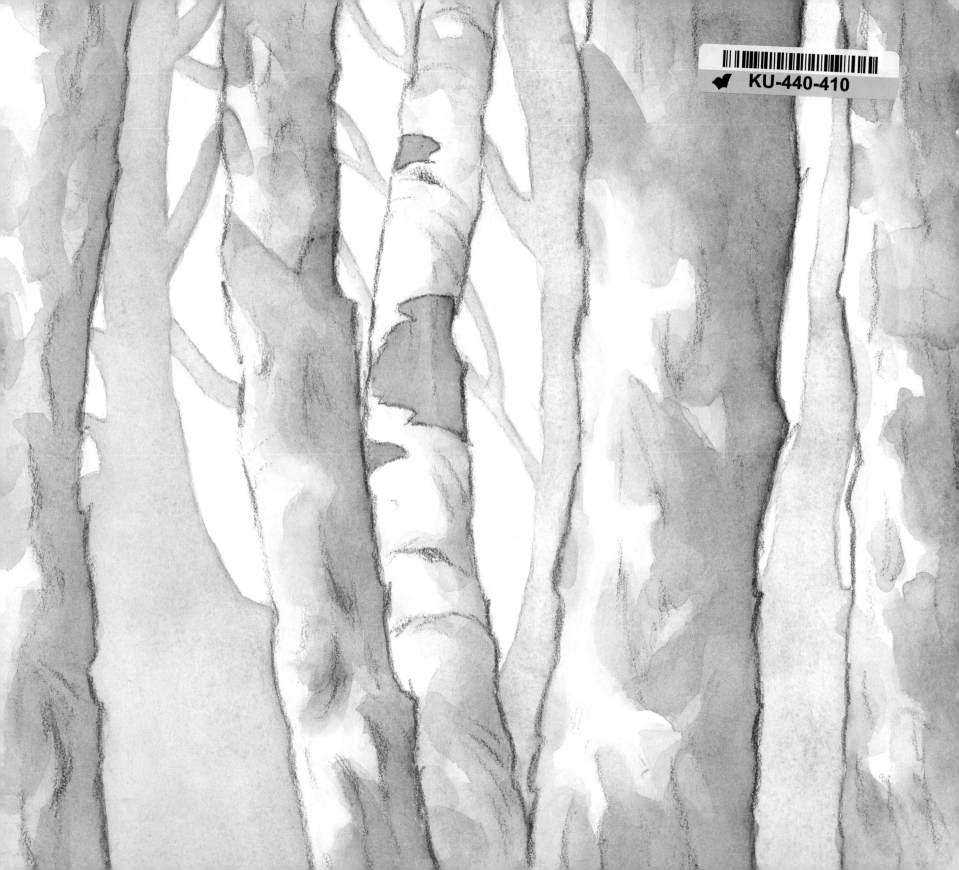

To Louis
~ C L

To John, Libby, Devan, Meggy and Katie
~ A E

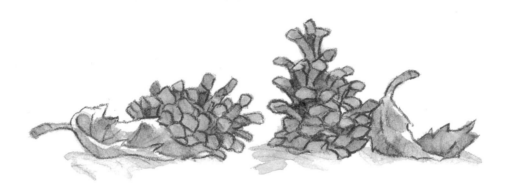

LITTLE TIGER PRESS
An imprint of Magi Publications
1 The Coda Centre, 189 Munster Road, London SW6 6AW
www.littletigerpress.com

First published in Great Britain 2005

This edition published 2006

A CIP catalogue record for this book is available from the British Library

Printed in Belgium by Proost N.V.

2 4 6 8 10 9 7 5 3 1

Too Busy for Benjie

Christine Leeson

Andy Ellis

Little Tiger Press
London

Benjie Beaver's family
were always busy. Gnawing
and building, they worked when
the sun was shining and they
worked when it rained.

No one ever seemed to have the
time to play with Benjie.

"Mum, will you play with me?" Benjie
asked one warm summer day.
"Sorry, love, I'm busy," said Mother Beaver.
"You could help me gnaw down this willow tree."
But gnawing didn't sound like much fun.
"Er . . . I'll come back later," said Benjie
and paddled off down the river.

Another day Benjie ran up to his father.

  "Will you play catch with me?" he asked.

  "Sorry, son," said Father Beaver. "I'm collecting
pine branches for our winter home. You could
always help me."

  But collecting branches didn't sound
very exciting. "Umm . . . never mind,"
Benjie mumbled, and hurried
into the forest.

"Will you play with me?" Benjie asked his big sister Bess one windy autumn morning. "Why don't you be useful and take this maple branch to our winter store?" Bess tutted. "We don't all have time for playing about, you know."

But Benjie had already swished away through the fallen leaves. His sister wasn't much fun today.

The weather grew colder and ice
came to nip the beavers' busy paws.
  "Yippee!" shouted Benjie, stretching
up to catch the first flakes of falling snow.
   It was time for the beaver family to
stop working. Their winter home
was ready at last.

The days passed. Outside, the world sparkled and crackled with frost. Inside, the beavers were very cosy . . . and very bored.

One day, as Mum brought some willow branches from their winter store, Benjie said, "I remember the day you got those . . ."

  "I don't suppose you were doing anything useful," snorted Bess.

    But Mum said, "Why don't you tell us about it, Benjie?"

So Benjie told them about splashing
in the cool stream, playing tickle feather
with the ducks.
 "That sounds like fun," smiled Mum.
 "We could play tickle feather now!"
said Benjie.

So the beavers played all
afternoon until they were
out of breath with laughter.
"I suppose that was quite
good fun," said Bess.

"This snow is lasting for ever!" groaned
Dad the next day as he swam in with
a pine branch.
"It was hot the day you cut that
branch," said Benjie.
"And I suppose you were
playing around again,"
yawned Bess.
But Dad said,
"I'd like to hear all
about it, Benjie."

So Benjie told them of
his day chasing through
the sunny forest, playing
hunt the pine cone with
the squirrels.

 "I haven't played that
game since I was small,"
said Dad.

 "Let's play now!"
said Benjie.

So the beavers played
hunt the pine cone until
long past their bedtime.

On another long day
Bess said, "So, Benjie, what
were you up to while I was
collecting this maple log?"
 "I was busy too!" said
Benjie. "I was gathering
twigs. But then I saw
some big, scary bears!
I hid behind a tree and
watched them eat honey."
 "How exciting!" gasped
Bess. "Let's all play
scary bears!"

So the beavers played scary
bears until they could hardly stand.
"That was great, Benjie!" giggled
Bess, sleepily.

All through the grey winter days
Benjie told stories and made up games.
Each one brightened the darkness
of their cosy little home.
   Then, at last, the ice began to melt.
The beavers swam out into a fresh
spring morning.

Dad looked at their home.
It had been battered by the
winter winds.

"Dear me!" he said. "This
place needs repairs. Come on,
everyone! Let's get busy!"

Benjie began to collect branches. Then he paused, gazing at the flowers blowing in the breeze.

Dad smiled. "Maybe we don't
have to start work right away," he said.
 "Hooray!" shouted Bess. "Now we
can play!"
    And Benjie and his family played
together in the warm spring
sunshine.

More books to keep you busy from Little Tiger Press

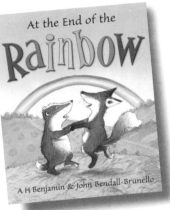

At the End of the **Rainbow**
A H Benjamin & John Bendall-Brunello

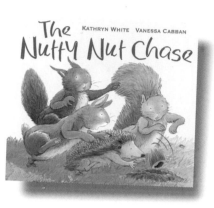

KATHRYN WHITE VANESSA CABBAN
The **Nutty Nut Chase**

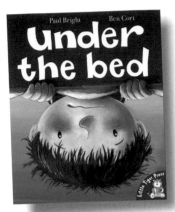

Paul Bright   Ben Cort
Under the bed

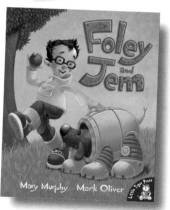

Foley and Jem
Mary Murphy   Mark Oliver

Claire Freedman and Daniel Howarth
The **Busy-Busy-Day**

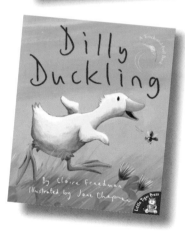

Dilly Duckling
By Claire Freedman
Illustrated by Jane Chapman

For information regarding any of the above titles or
for our catalogue, please contact us:

Little Tiger Press, 1 The Coda Centre,

189 Munster Road, London SW6 6AW

Tel: 020 7385 6333 Fax: 020 7385 7333

E-mail: info@littletiger.co.uk

www.littletigerpress.com